EASY PIANO

My First Christmas Song Book

A TREASURY OF FAVORITE SONGS TO PLAY

CONTENTS:

Cover photo © Richard Gaul / Getty Images

ISBN 978-1-4803-4585-0

HAL • LEONARD®
CORPORATION

7777 W. BLUEMOUND RD. P.O. BOX 13819 MILWAUKEE, WI 53213

Visit Hal Leonard Online at
www.halleonard.com

Caroling, Caroling

Words by WIHLA HUTSON
Music by ALFRED BURT

Christmas Time Is Here

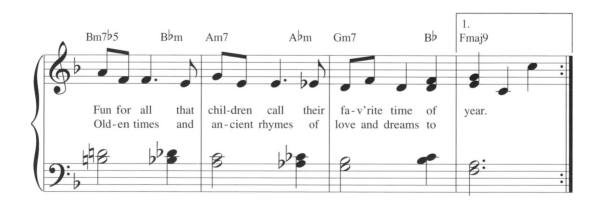

Words by LEE MENDELSON
Music by VINCE GUARALDI

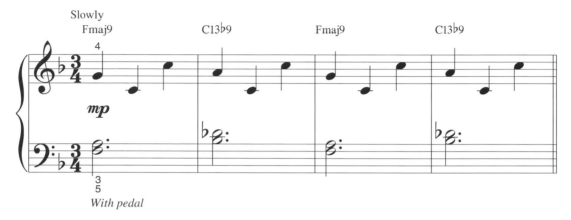

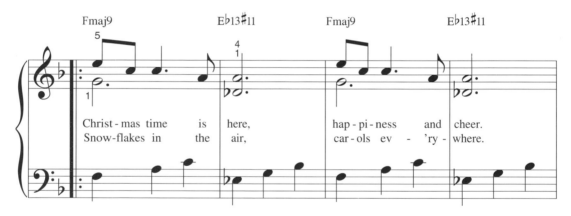

Christ - mas time   is   here,   hap - pi - ness   and   cheer.
Snow-flakes in   the   air,   car - ols ev - 'ry - where.

Fun for all   that   chil - dren call   their   fa - v'rite time of   year.
Old-en times   and   an - cient rhymes   of   love and dreams to

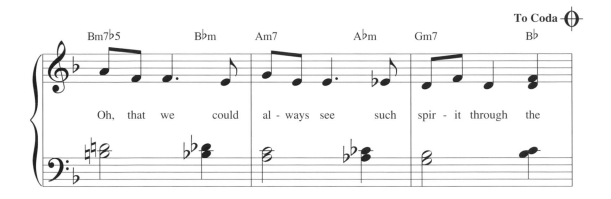

Bm7♭5   B♭m   Am7   A♭m   Gm7   B♭   **To Coda** ⊕

Oh, that we could al - ways see such spir - it through the

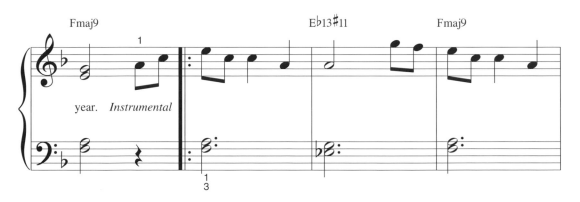

Fmaj9   E♭13♯11   Fmaj9

year. *Instrumental*

E♭13♯11   Bm7♭5   B♭m   Am7   A♭m   Gm7   B♭

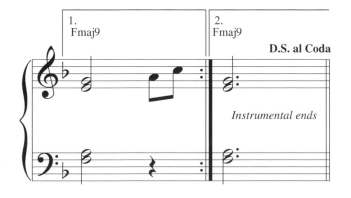

1.
Fmaj9

2.
Fmaj9

D.S. al Coda

Instrumental ends

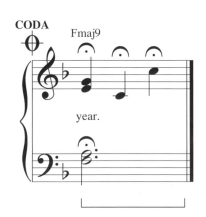

CODA ⊕   Fmaj9

year.

6

The Christmas Song
(Chestnuts Roasting on an Open Fire)

Music and Lyric by MEL TORME
and ROBERT WELLS

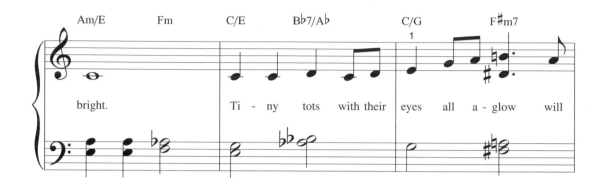

bright. Ti - ny tots with their eyes all a - glow will

find it hard to sleep to - night. They know that San - ta's on his

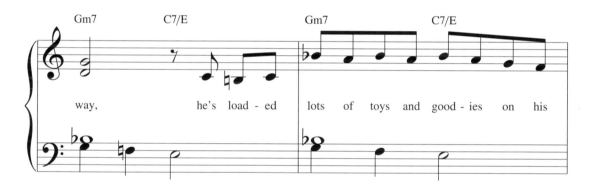

way, he's load - ed lots of toys and good - ies on his

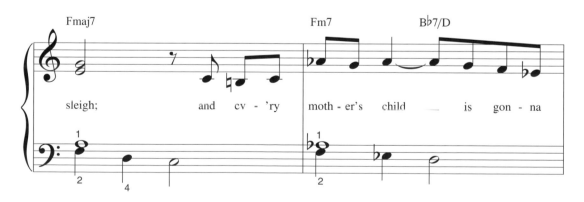

sleigh; and ev - 'ry moth - er's child is gon - na

spy _____ to see if rein-deer real-ly know how to

fly. And so, I'm of-fer-ing this sim-ple phrase to

kids from one to nine-ty - two: al-though it's been said man-y

times, man-y ways, Mer-ry Christ-mas to you.

rit.

FROSTY THE SNOW MAN

Words and Music by STEVE NELSON
and JACK ROLLINS

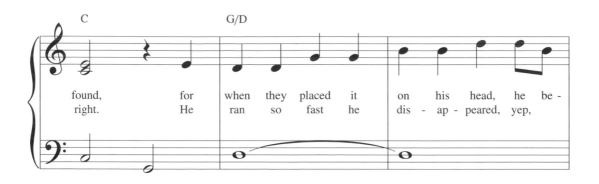

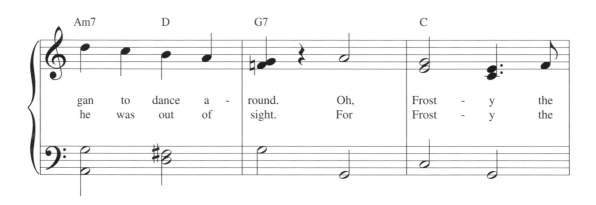

HAPPY HOLIDAY

Words and Music by
IRVING BERLIN

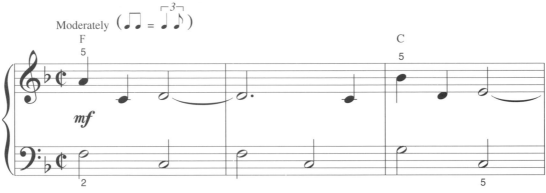

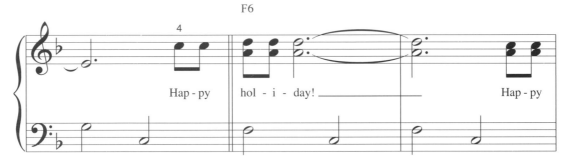

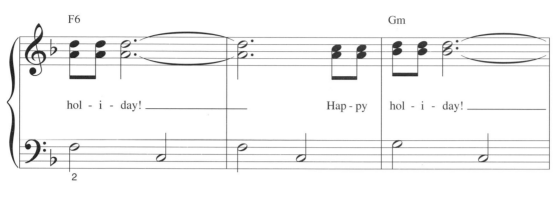

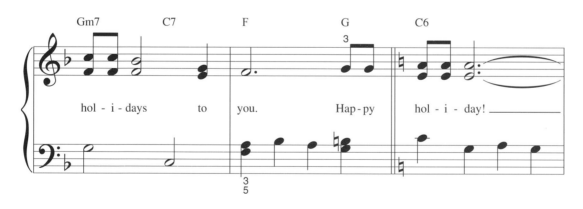

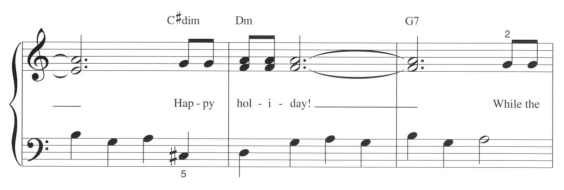

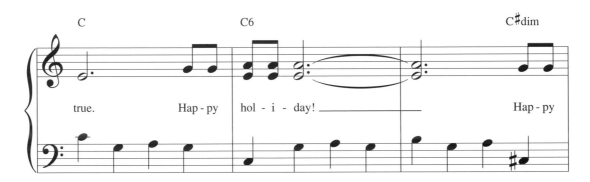

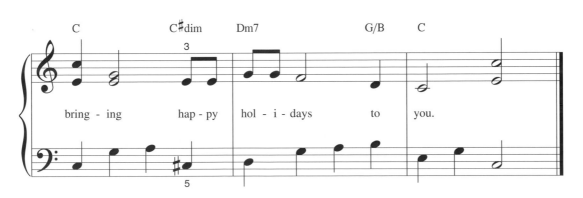

Have Yourself a Merry Little Christmas

Words and Music by HUGH MARTIN
and RALPH BLANE

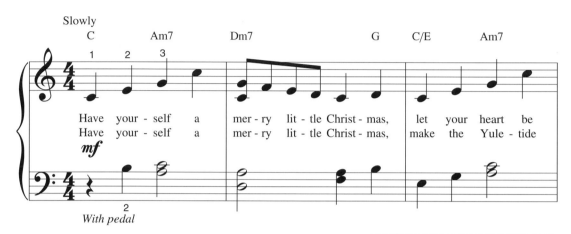

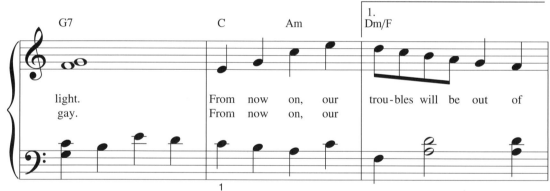

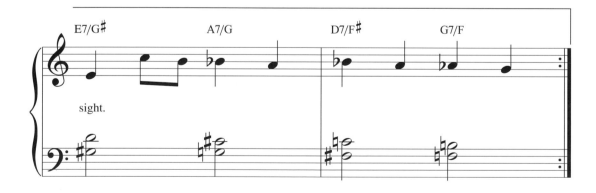

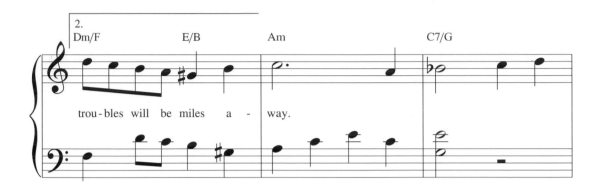

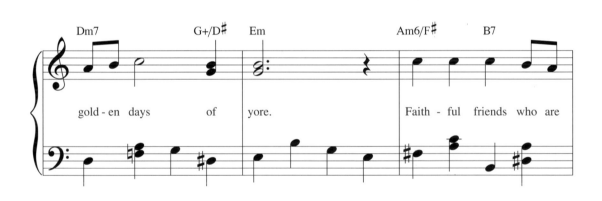

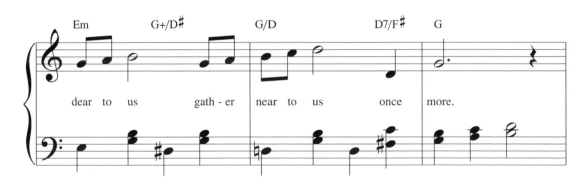

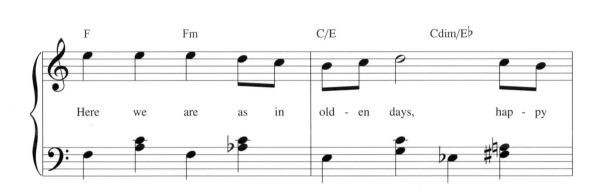

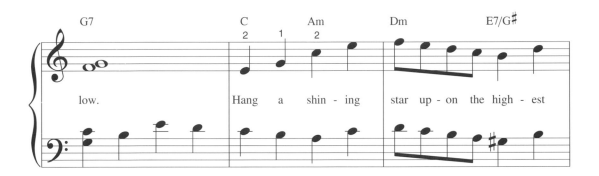

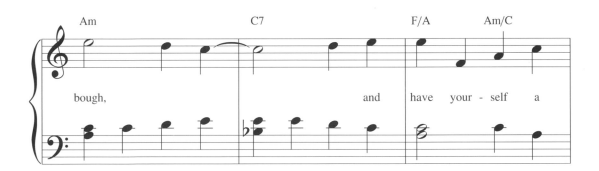

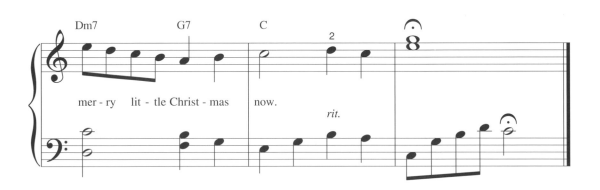

Here Comes Santa Claus
(Right Down Santa Claus Lane)

Words and Music by GENE AUTRY
and OAKLEY HALDEMAN

Moderately bright

Here comes San - ta Claus! Here comes San - ta Claus!

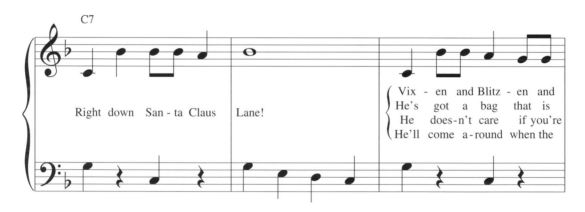

Right down San - ta Claus Lane!

Vix - en and Blitz - en and
He's got a bag that is
He does-n't care if you're
He'll come a - round when the

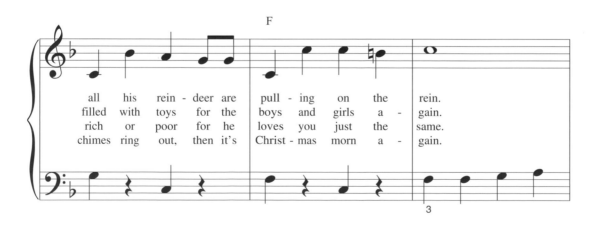

all his rein - deer are pull - ing on the rein.
filled with toys for the boys and girls a - gain.
rich or poor for he loves you just the same.
chimes ring out, then it's Christ - mas morn a - gain.

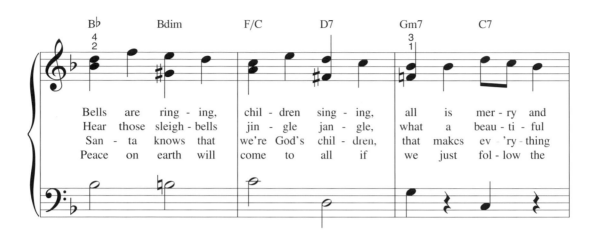

Bells   are   ring - ing,   chil - dren   sing - ing,   all   is   mer - ry   and
Hear   those   sleigh - bells   jin - gle   jan - gle,   what   a   beau - ti - ful
San - ta   knows   that   we're   God's   chil - dren,   that   makes   ev - 'ry - thing
Peace   on   earth   will   come   to   all   if   we   just   fol - low   the

bright.   Hang   your   stock - ings   and   say   your   pray'rs,
sight.   Jump   in   bed,   cov - er   up   your   head,   } 'cause
right.   Fill   your   hearts   with   a   Christ - mas   cheer,
light.   Let's   give   thanks   to   the   Lord   a - bove,

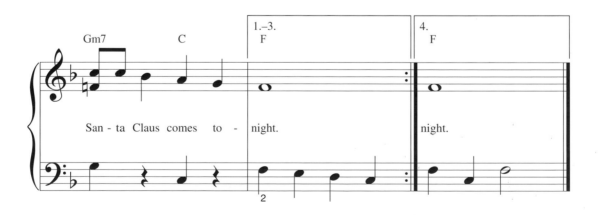

San - ta   Claus   comes   to - night.   night.

A Holly Jolly Christmas

Music and Lyrics by
JOHNNY MARKS

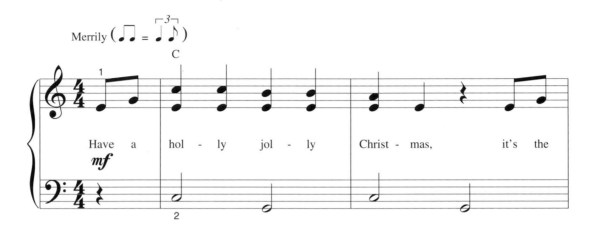

Have a hol-ly jol-ly Christ-mas, it's the

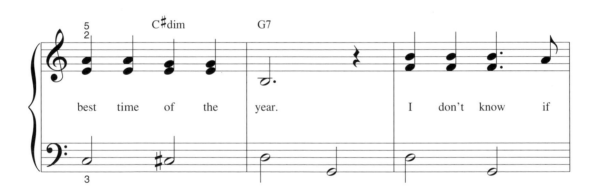

best time of the year. I don't know if

there'll be snow, but let's all give a cheer. Have a

C#dim

hol - ly jol - ly Christ - mas and when you walk down the

G7

street, say hel - lo to friends you know and

C   F

ev - 'ry - one you meet.   Oh,   ho,   the

Em7   F   C

mis - tle - toe hung where you can see.

24

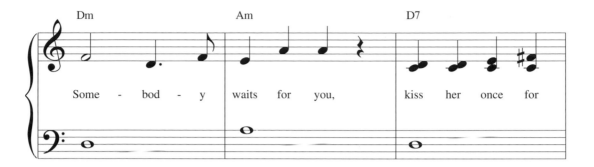

Some - bod - y waits for you, kiss her once for

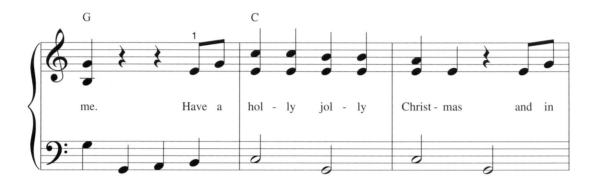

me. Have a hol - ly jol - ly Christ - mas and in

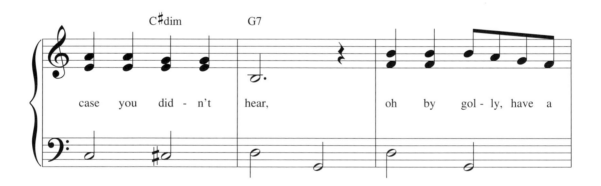

case you did - n't hear, oh by gol - ly, have a

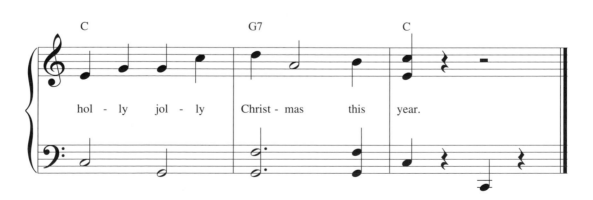

hol - ly jol - ly Christ - mas this year.

I Saw Mommy Kissing Santa Claus

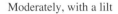

Words and Music by
TOMMIE CONNOR

Moderately, with a lilt

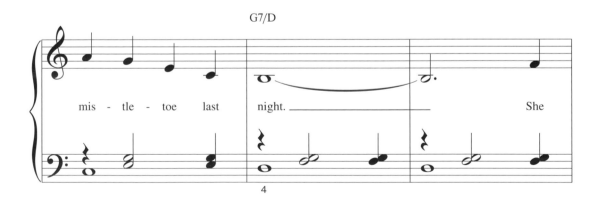

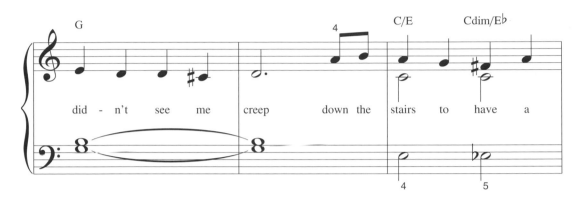

did - n't see me creep down the stairs to have a

peek; she thought that I was tucked up in my

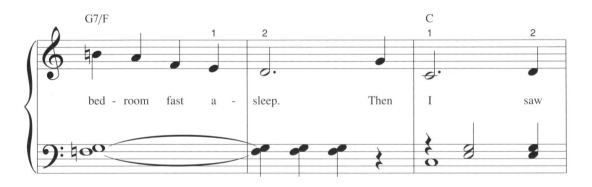

bed - room fast a - sleep. Then I saw

Mom - my tick - le San - ta Claus

I'll Be Home for Christmas

Words and Music by KIM GANNON
and WALTER KENT

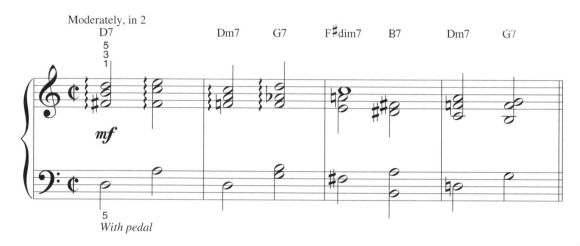

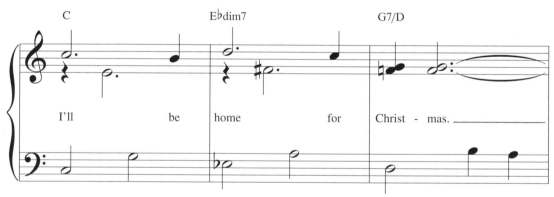

I'll   be   home   for   Christ - mas. _____

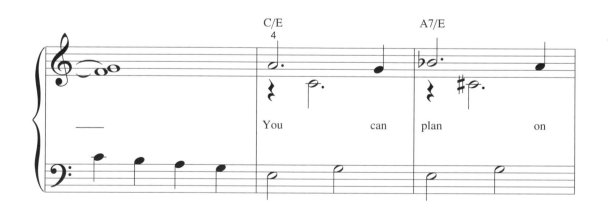

_____   You   can   plan   on

where the love - light gleams. I'll be home for Christ - mas, if on - ly in my dreams.

rit.

It's Beginning to Look Like Christmas

By MEREDITH WILLSON

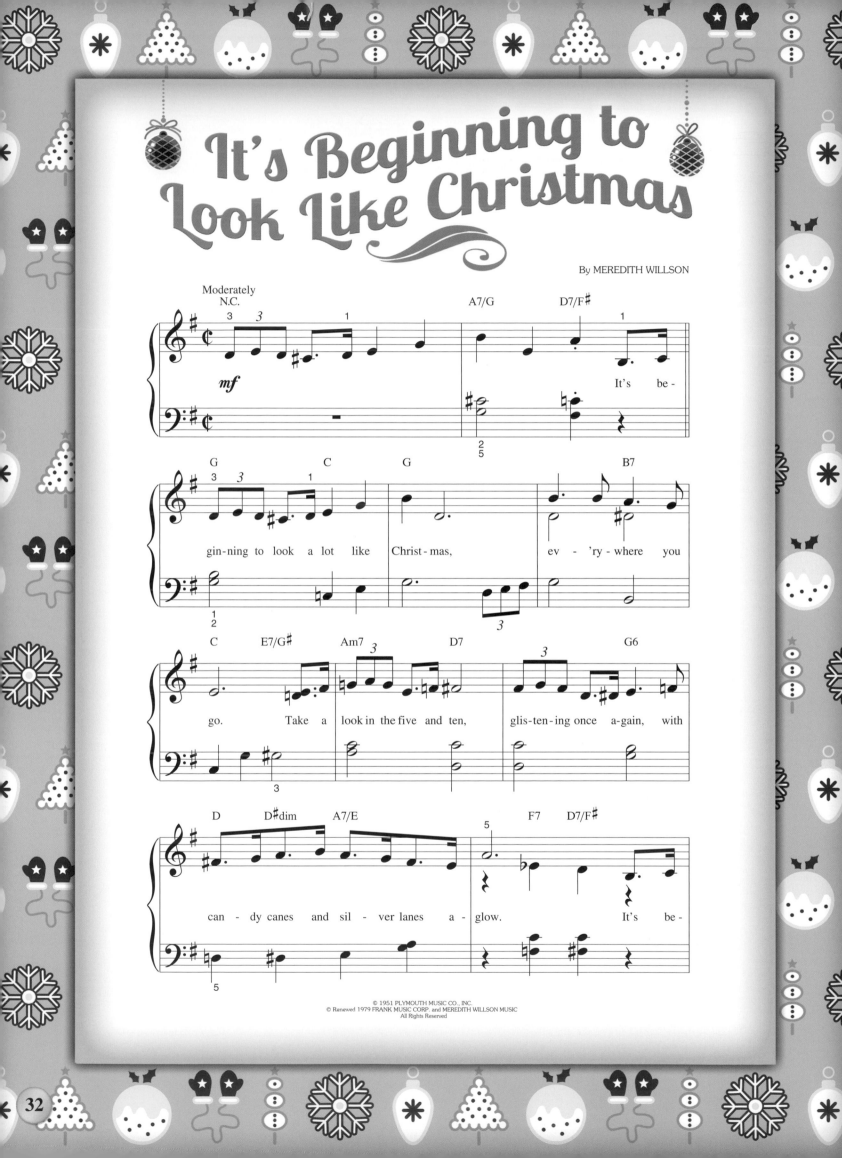

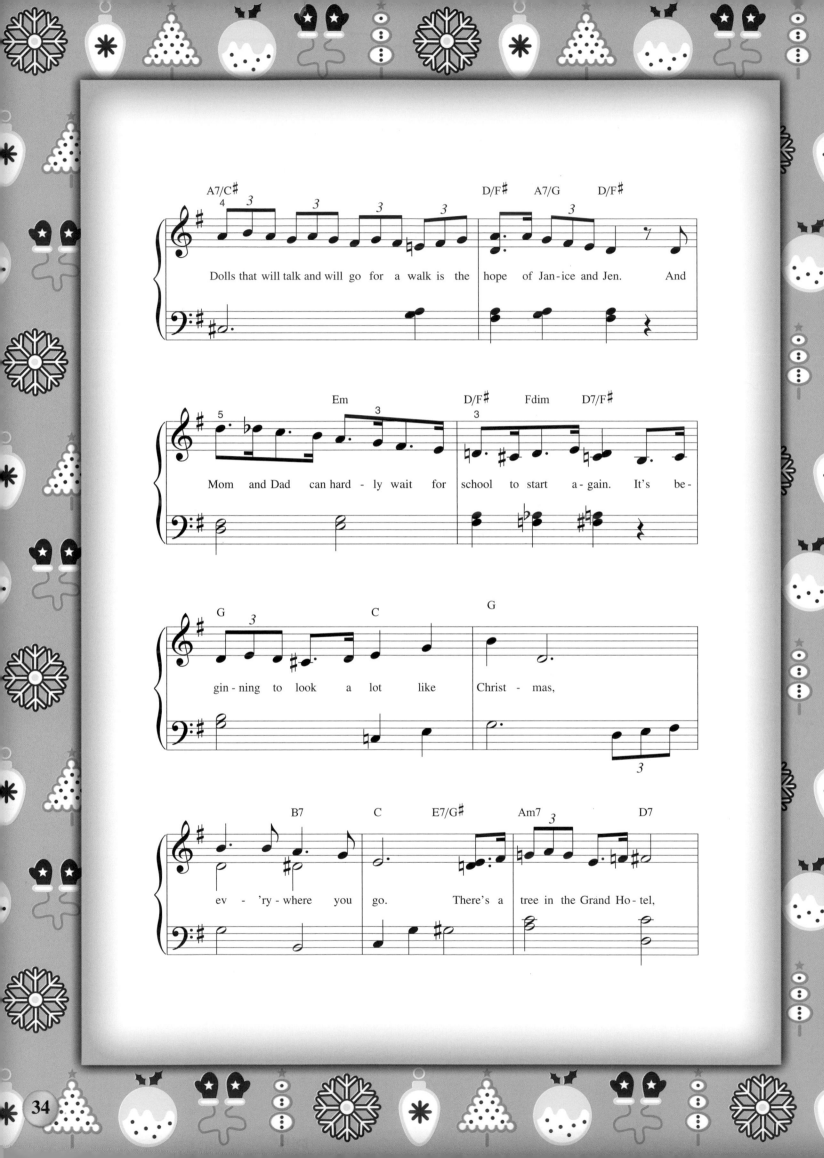

Let It Snow! Let It Snow! Let It Snow!

Words by SAMMY CAHN
Music by JULE STYNE

hate go-ing out in the storm; but if you'll real-ly hold me tight,

all the way home I'll be warm. The fire is slow-ly dy-ing, and my

dear, we're still good - bye-ing, but as long as you love me

so, let it snow, let it snow, let it snow.

THE LITTLE DRUMMER BOY

Words and Music by HARRY SIMEONE, HENRY ONORATI and KATHERINE DAVIS

"Come," they told me, pa-
Lit - tle Ba - by, pa-

rum pum pum pum, _____
rum pum pum pum, _____

a new - born
I am a

King to see, pa - rum pum pum pum.
poor boy, too, pa - rum pum pum pum.

Our fin - est gifts we bring, pa - rum pum pum pum, _____
I have no gift to bring, pa - rum pum pum pum, _____

A Marshmallow World

Words by CARL SIGMAN
Music by PETER DE ROSE

With a lilt

It's a marsh - mal - low world in the win - ter _____ when the
marsh - mal - low clouds be - ing friend - ly _____ in the

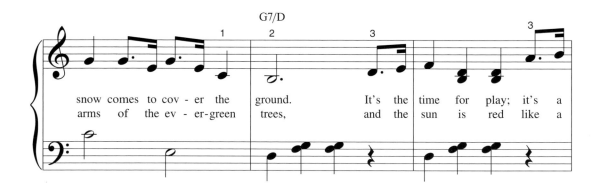

snow comes to cov - er the ground. It's the time for play; it's a
arms of the ev - er - green trees, and the sun is red like a

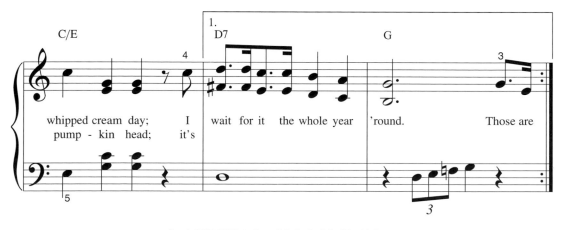

whipped cream day; I wait for it the whole year 'round. Those are
pump - kin head; it's

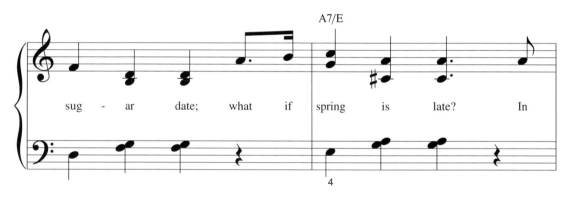

Rudolph the Red-Nosed Reindeer

Music and Lyrics by
JOHNNY MARKS

Then how the rein-deer loved him, as they shout-ed out with glee,

"Ru-dolph the red-nosed rein - deer, you'll go down in his - to -

ry!" You'll go down in his - to -

ry! _____

The Most Wonderful Day of the Year

Music and Lyrics by
JOHNNY MARKS

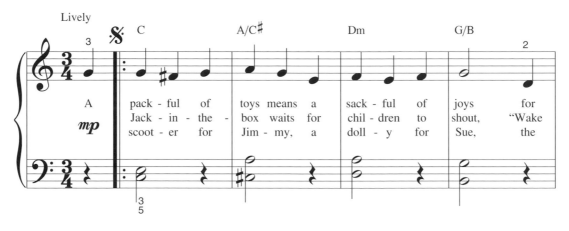

Lively

A
pack - ful of toys means a sack - ful of joys for
Jack - in - the - box waits for chil - dren to shout, "Wake
scoot - er for Jim - my, a doll - y for Sue, the

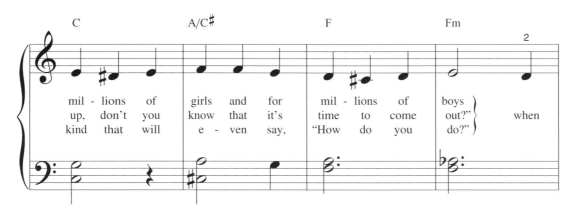

mil - lions of girls and for mil - lions of boys
up, don't you know that it's time to come out?" when
kind that will e - ven say, "How do you do?"

Christ - mas Day is here, _____ the most

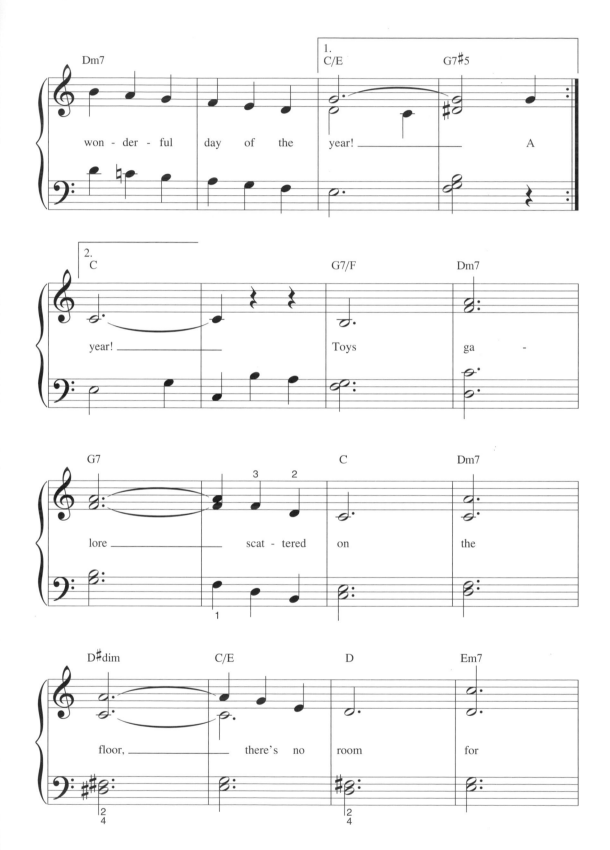

more, _____ and it's all be - cause of

CODA

Sanー - ta Claus! A won - der - ful,

rall. *a tempo*

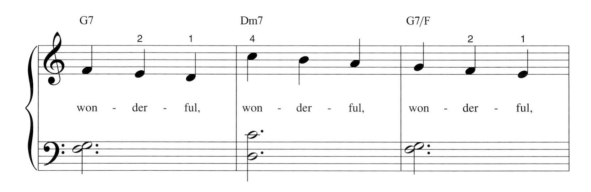

won - der - ful, won - der - ful, won - der - ful,

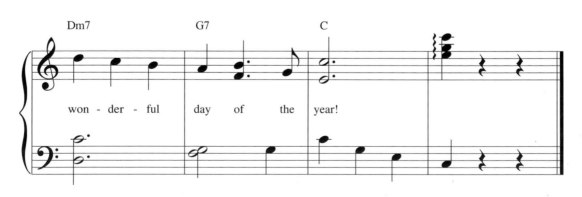

won - der - ful day of the year!

Rockin' Around the Christmas Tree

Music and Lyrics by
JOHNNY MARKS

Moderate Rock

Rock-in' a - round the Christ-mas tree ___ at the Christ-mas par-ty hop. ___

Mis - tle - toe hung where you can see ___ ev -'ry

cou - ple tries to stop. Rock-in' a - round the

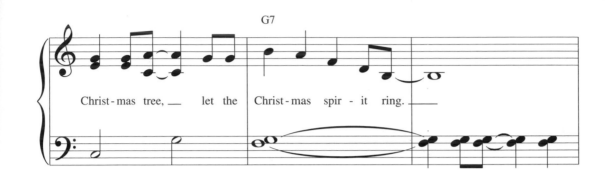

Christ-mas tree, ___ let the Christ-mas spir-it ring. ___

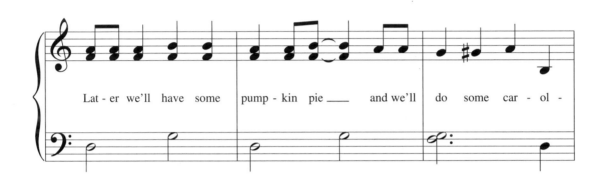

Lat-er we'll have some pump-kin pie ___ and we'll do some car-ol-

ing. You will get a sen-ti-men-tal feel-ing when you

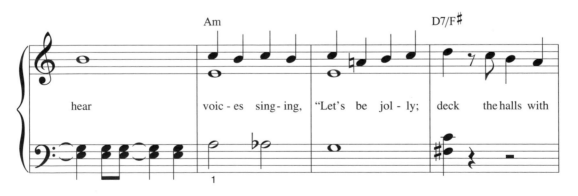

hear voic-es sing-ing, "Let's be jol-ly; deck the halls with

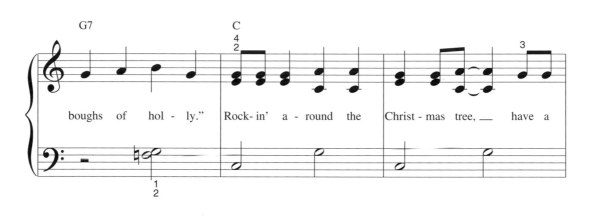

boughs of hol - ly." Rock- in' a - round the Christ - mas tree, ___ have a

hap - py hol - i - day. ___ Ev -'ry - one danc - ing

mer - ri - ly ___ in the new old fash - ioned

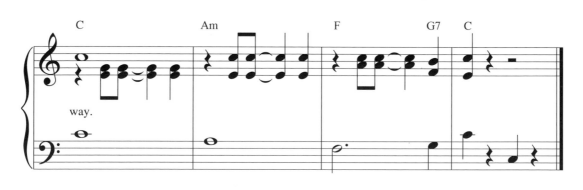

way.

Sleigh Ride

Music by LEROY ANDERSON
Words by MITCHELL PARISH

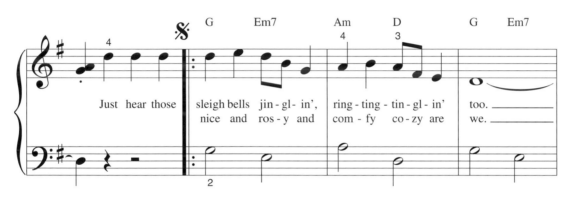

Just hear those sleigh bells jin-gl-in', ring-ting-tin-gl-in' too. _____
nice and ros-y and com-fy co-zy are we. _____

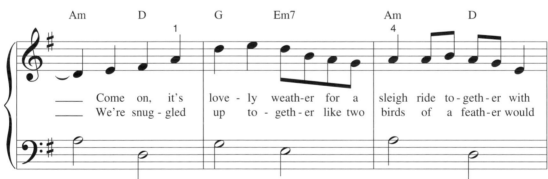

_____ Come on, it's love-ly weath-er for a sleigh ride to-geth-er with
_____ We're snug-gled up to-geth-er like two birds of a feath-er would

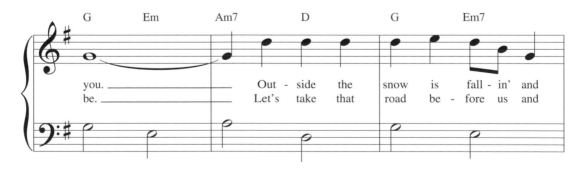

you. _____ Out-side the snow is fall-in' and
be. _____ Let's take that road be-fore us and

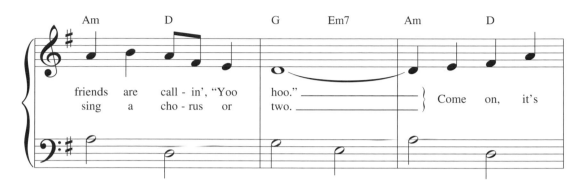

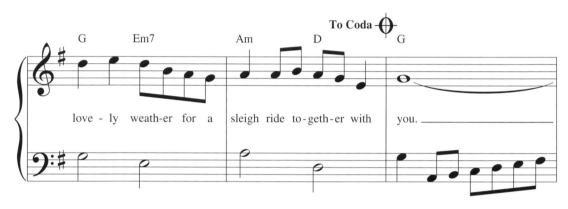

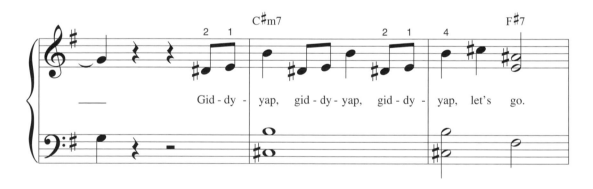

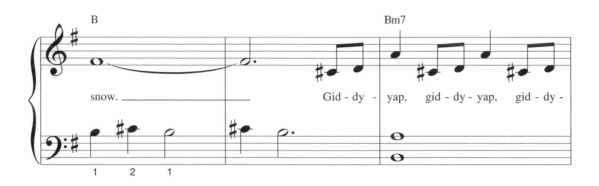

snow. _____ Gid - dy - yap, gid - dy - yap, gid - dy -

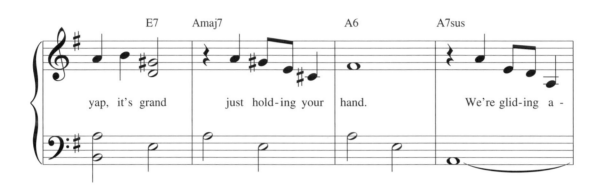

yap, it's grand   just hold-ing your   hand.   We're glid-ing a -

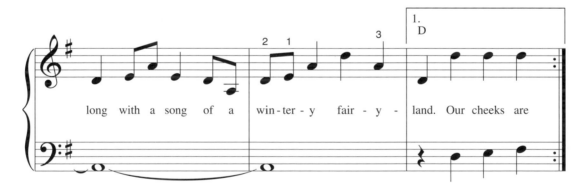

long   with   a   song   of   a   win - ter - y   fair - y -   land. Our cheeks are

land. Our cheeks are

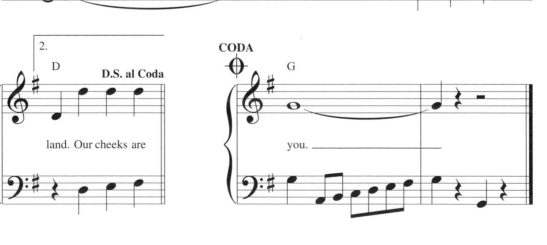

you. _____

Silver Bells

Words and Music by JAY LIVINGSTON
and RAY EVANS

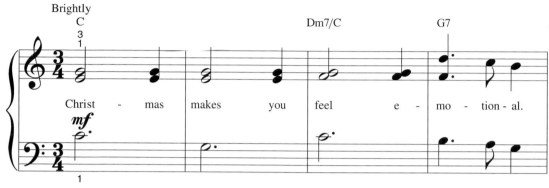

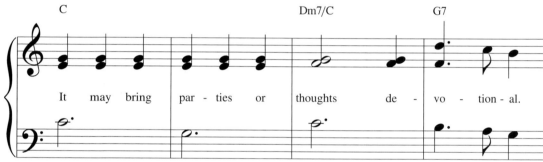

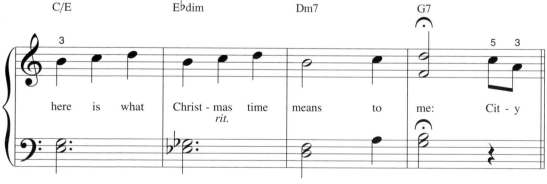

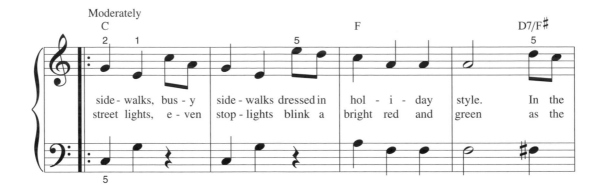

side - walks, bus - y side - walks dressed in hol - i - day style. In the
street lights, e - ven stop-lights blink a bright red and green as the

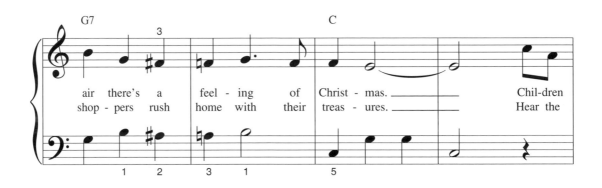

air there's a feel - ing of Christ - mas. _____ Chil-dren
shop - pers rush home with their treas - ures. _____ Hear the

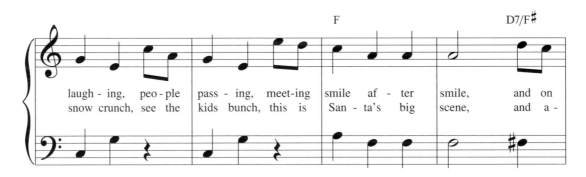

laugh - ing, peo - ple pass - ing, meet-ing smile af - ter smile, and on
snow crunch, see the kids bunch, this is San - ta's big scene, and a -

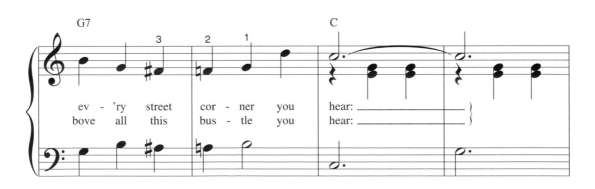

ev - 'ry street cor - ner you hear: _____
bove all this bus - tle you hear: _____

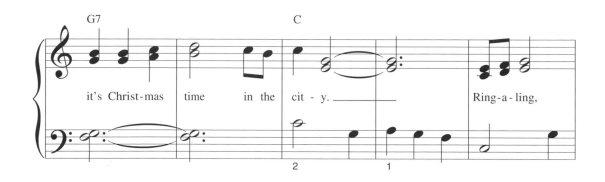

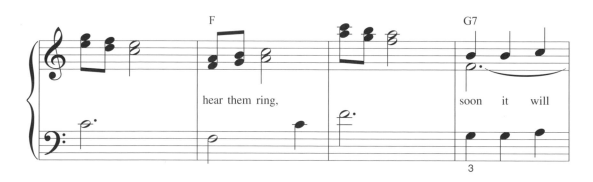

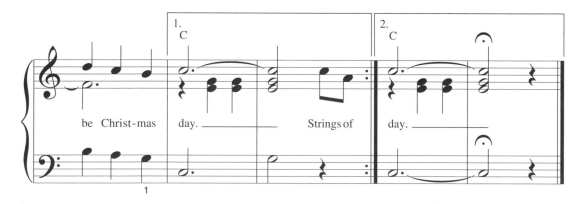

Santa Claus Is Comin' to Town

Words by HAVEN GILLESPIE
Music by J. FRED COOTS

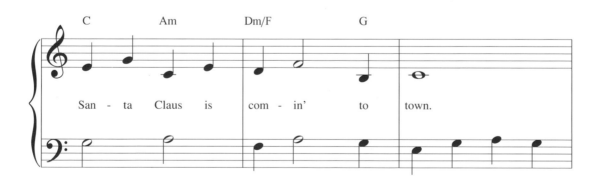

He's   mak-ing a list   and   check-ing it twice,

gon - na find out who's   naugh-ty and nice,   San - ta Claus is

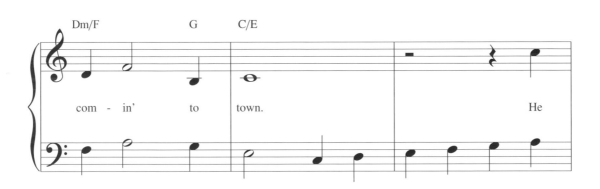

com - in'   to   town.   He

sees you when you're   sleep - in',   he   knows when you're a -

wake,   he   knows   if   you've   been   bad   or   good,   so   be

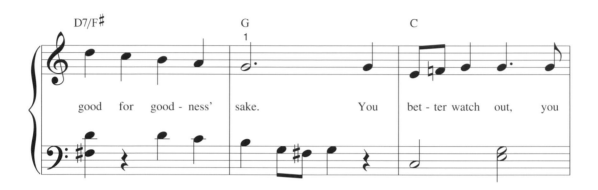

good   for   good - ness'   sake.   You   bet - ter   watch   out,   you

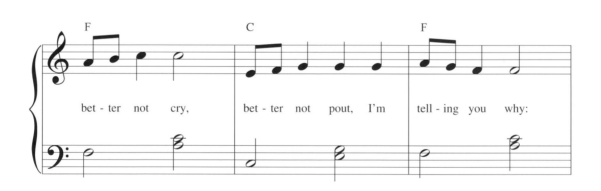

bet - ter   not   cry,   bet - ter   not   pout,   I'm   tell - ing   you   why:

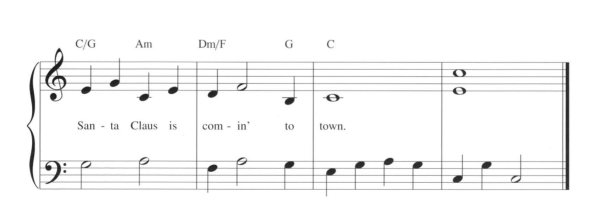

San - ta   Claus   is   com - in'   to   town.

WINTER WONDERLAND

Words by DICK SMITH
Music by FELIX BERNARD

Sleigh-bells ring, are you list-'nin'? In the lane snow is

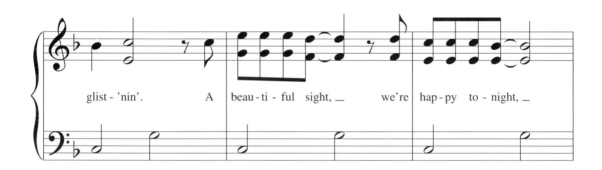

glist-'nin'. A beau-ti-ful sight, __ we're hap-py to-night, __

walk-in' in a win-ter won-der-land. Gone a-way is the

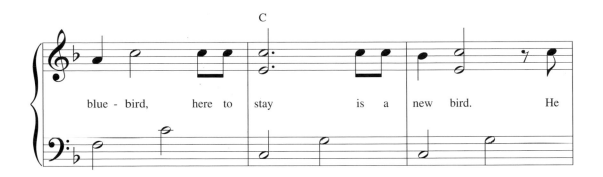

blue - bird,   here to   stay   is   a   new   bird.   He

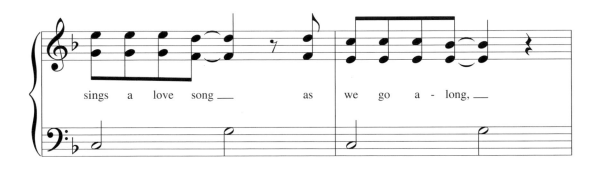

sings   a   love   song ___   as   we   go   a - long, ___

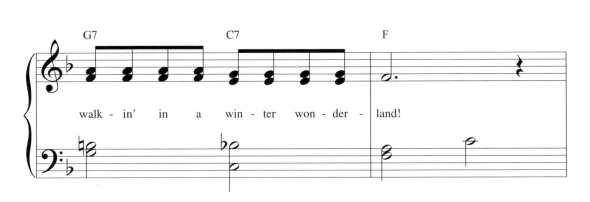

walk - in'   in   a   win - ter   won - der - land!

In   the   mead - ow   we   can   build   a   snow - man,
In   the   mead - ow   we   can   build   a   snow - man,

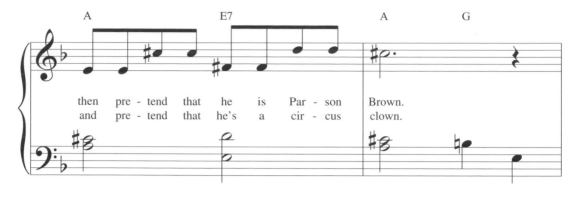

then pre - tend that he is Par - son Brown.
and pre - tend that he's a cir - cus clown.

He'll say, "Are you mar - ried?" We'll say, "No, man! But
We'll have lots of fun with Mis - ter Snow - man un -

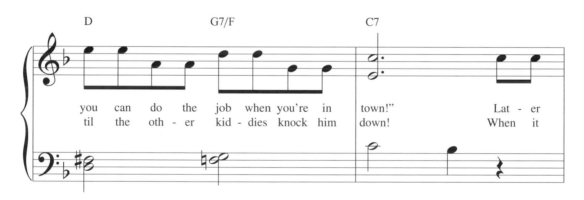

you can do the job when you're in town!" Lat - er
til the oth - er kid - dies knock him down! When it

on we'll con - spire, ___ as we dream by the
snows, it's so thrill - in', though your nose gets a

fire, _____ to face un - a - fraid _____ the
chill - in'. We frol - ic and play _____ the

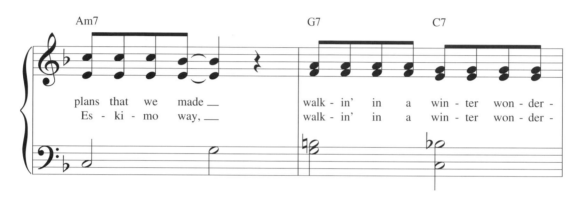

Am7   G7   C7

plans that we made _____ walk - in' in a win - ter won - der -
Es - ki - mo way, _____ walk - in' in a win - ter won - der -

1. F   2. F   D7   G7   C7

land!   Sleigh-bells   land,   walk - in' in a win - ter won - der -

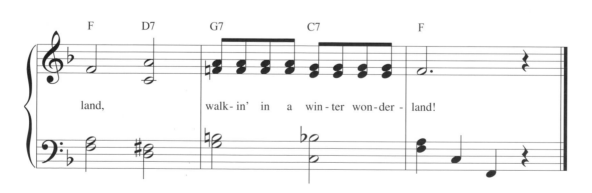

F   D7   G7   C7   F

land,   walk - in' in a win - ter won - der - land!

© JanuaryFrost / Alamy

White Christmas

Words and Music by
IRVING BERLIN

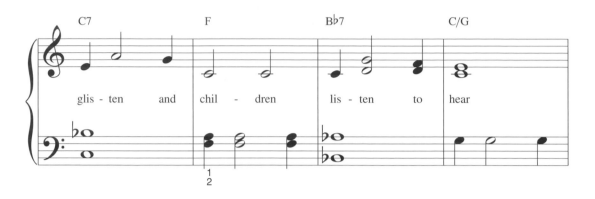

glis - ten and chil - dren lis - ten to hear

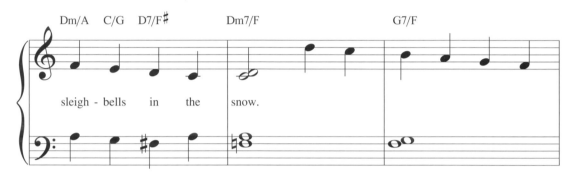

sleigh - bells in the snow.

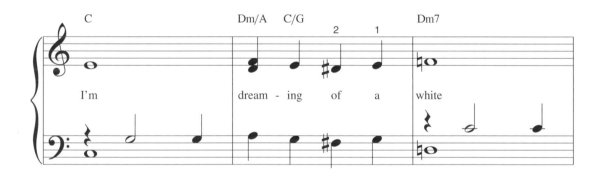

I'm dream - ing of a white

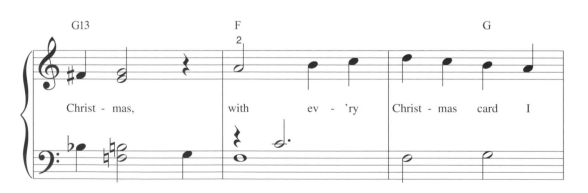

Christ - mas, with ev - 'ry Christ - mas card I

write: _____ "May your days be

mer - ry and bright _____ and may all your

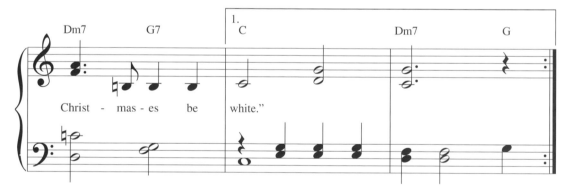

Christ - mas - es be white."

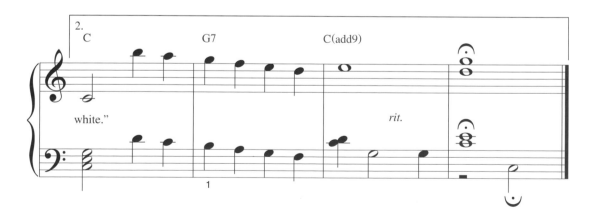

white." *rit.*

Suzy Snowflake

Words and Music by SID TEPPER
and ROY BENNETT

Happily

Here comes Suz - y Snow - flake

dressed in a snow-white gown, tap tap tap-pin' at your

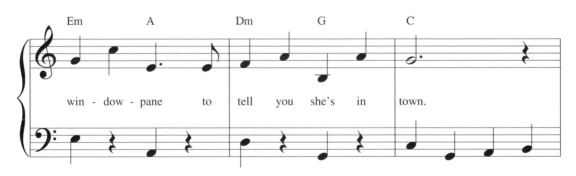

win - dow - pane to tell you she's in town.

Here comes Suz - y Snow - flake, soon you will hear her

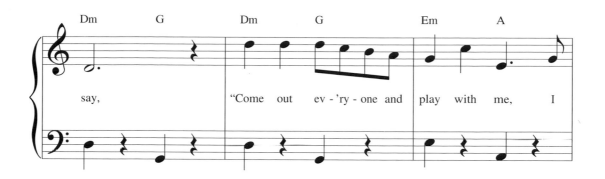

say,   "Come out ev-'ry-one and   play with me,   I

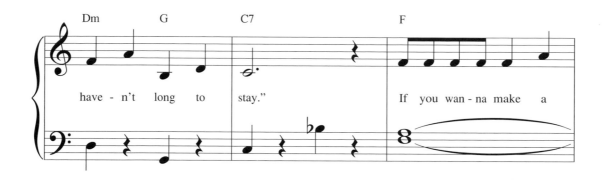

have-n't   long   to   stay."   If you wan-na make   a

snow - man,   I'll help you make one,   one, two, three.

If you wan-na take   a   sleigh   ride,   then   the ride's on

me.   Here   comes   Suz - y Snow-flake,   look at her tum - blin'

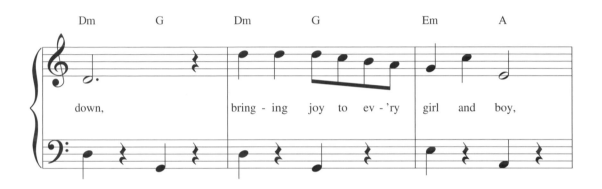

down,   bring - ing   joy to ev - 'ry   girl and boy,

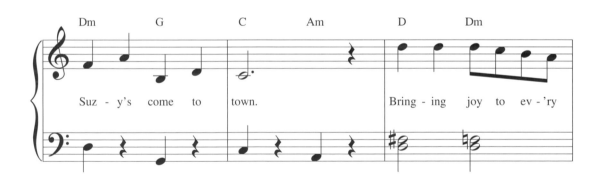

Suz - y's come to   town.   Bring - ing   joy to ev - 'ry

girl and boy,   Suz - y's come to   town.